CN00835639

A WORD ABOUT YOUR

HEALING

DON EGAN

Books by the same author:

Healing is coming!
Searching for Home - a journey of the soul.
Excess baggage - a new type of monasticism.
The Chronicles of Godfrey.
Beautiful on the Mountains - autobiography

older titles are available at
www.rsvptrust.co.uk

First published 2001.
Reprinted 2008.
Kindle Edition 2011.
Revised Edition 2015.

Create Space Edition.

ISBN-13: 978-1517101374
ISBN-10: 1517101379

A WORD ABOUT YOUR
HEALING

'...how God anointed Jesus of Nazareth with the Holy Spirit and power, and how he went around doing good and healing all who were under the power of the devil, because God was with him.'
Acts 10:38

Contents

one

The blind see, the lame walk!

I have written this book to help you get healed and stay healed. It comes from seeing incredible miracles of physical healing which set people free to live a full and active life. Alongside these miracles, I have also seen many people, including Christians, with long-standing illnesses, who seemed to have lost any hope of God healing them. Some have prayed so many times for healing without results, that their disappointment is now the biggest obstacle to their healing.

As I have applied the principles outlined in this book, I have seen many wonderful healings, mainly in others but also in my own body.

It began some years ago in Rwanda, during a ministry time, when a lady who had been blind for twelve years suddenly said she could see. Another young lady who had very poor vision for many years regained her full sight. A lady with crippling abdominal pain suddenly began touching her toes. In another meeting, as I was asking people to share any healings they had received, a man began dancing and leaping. When I asked the interpreter what he was doing, he told me that four men had carried this man to the meeting because he couldn't walk, but when I had prayed for healing in the meeting the previous night, he had been completely healed. A clergyman from Tanzania wrote to me after one of our missions to refugees.

Rusumo Parish

Ngara

TANZANIA

Dear Brother Don,

Greetings in the name of our Lord Jesus Christ. I would like to take this opportunity to thank you for the blessings you left with us during the September Mission in the Refugee Camp.

I have been receiving many testimonies from people who got healed from different diseases. e.g. my daughter who recovered her sight, my sister who had had a heart attack, one man and woman who were suffering for so many years with T.B. and were ready to die. Many in the camp got healed and continue giving their testimonies concerning the healing power of Jesus Christ.

Rev Canon Anania Nkware

Since then, sceptics have suggested that these types of dramatic healings only happen in Africa where people have a simple faith. However, as I applied the same principles in our UK meetings, the same dramatic results have occurred. Healing certainly requires faith but sophisticated Europeans are not excluded from exercising faith.

two

Simple but true

The principles in this book are simple but not simplistic. When I was attending high school, a boy once thumped me hard in the stomach with no warning. He stood there laughing. At first I couldn't breathe and certainly could not fight back. It took most of the rest of the day to fully recover. Satan comes at us like that sometimes. Suddenly from nowhere he sends a life threatening illness.

In the 1980's he did just that to my family. My mother suddenly became ill with a liver problem. Within two weeks she was dead. Our son was then born with several heart deformities and had to have heart surgery several times before his third birthday. My father then got cancer. He died within two weeks of the news. My son then died during surgery shortly before his third birthday. Spiritually it was just like being thumped in the stomach when you are totally unprepared. It took me many years to get over those things.

I have decided never to let that happen again. I want to be prepared for any attack of sickness in the future. If you have suffered in this sort of way, the devil will tell you that this book is trite nonsense and it won't work. That is a lie. The word of God is powerful and active and I have seen it heal many, many people including myself.

three

Avoid Organ Recitals

I used to belong to a prayer meeting where we prayed for the sick. Well, we were supposed to pray for the sick, but we tended to get organ recitals instead. It went something like this, 'Lord, we pray for Bill who has lung cancer. Lord, we pray for Gertrude who has failed kidneys. Lord, we pray for Fred with a bad heart. Lord, we pray for Sally with a damaged liver....'

And so it went on. We didn't pray in faith, because we focused on the diseased organs not on the Healer. We recited a list of organs - we had our own organ recital. We committed the mistake of the Israelites when faced with Goliath - we looked at the problem instead of the solution. David defeated Goliath because he focused on God's power and his word, not on the Goliath-size problem.

If you want to be healed, or to be used by God to heal others, then you need to learn what God says about healing. You need to focus on his word rather than the problem. You need to remove from your mind and heart all the lies about healing that you may have accepted by basing your understanding of healing on opinion, speculation and the devil's lies. You need to start over again by coming back to the word of God.

'In the beginning was the Word, and the Word was with God, and the Word was God.'

(John 1:1).

We have to look at ourselves and come fresh to what God says, refusing to dismiss his word but rather submitting ourselves to it.

The scriptures contained in this book are the most important ingredient because the word will bring life and health to your flesh.

'My [child], give attention to my words; Incline your ear to my sayings. Do not let them depart from your eyes; Keep them in the midst of your heart; For they are life to those who find them, And health to all their flesh.'

(Proverbs 4:20-22).

four

Be like Jesus...

I used to think that the ministry of Jesus was in a class of its own. I assumed that I could never really expect to see the things that Jesus did happening in my ministry. However, Jesus did not believe that his ministry was in a class of its own and he expected that I would see the same things happening in my ministry as happened in his. Before you accuse me of blasphemy, listen to Jesus.

'Most assuredly, I say to you, he who believes in me, the works that I do he will do also; and greater works than these he will do, because I go to My Father.'

(John 14:12)

The condition is: 'he who believes in me'. So we should not only expect to see the kind of miracles Jesus saw but even 'greater works'. As you grasp the principles in this book I pray that you will develop your faith and expectancy and receive all the blessings God has in store for you. And it doesn't really matter who you are because God is no respecter of persons.

'Then Peter opened his mouth, and said, 'Of a truth I perceive that God is no respecter of persons:"

(Acts 10:34 KJV)

It doesn't matter what we have done or not done in the past. As we present ourselves to God, ready to submit to his word, the Holy Spirit can minister to us for healing.

God is available to everyone, everywhere, all of the time.

five

Where does sickness come from?

If you are going to get healed, you will have to believe that God is good. It sounds simple but some people say 'God has put this sickness on me to teach me a lesson.' As though God is good but God is bad. That really is blasphemy. In any case, if you thought God was trying to teach you a lesson by putting sickness on you, why are you going to the doctor to escape from what you say is God's will? It just doesn't make sense.

There is a great deal of confusion about where sickness comes from. This confusion is a great hindrance to us receiving our healing. God made the situation very clear when Jesus said,

'The thief comes only to steal and kill and destroy; I have come that they may have life, and have it to the full.'

(John 10:10).

The thief Jesus is talking about is Satan. His plan is clear. He comes to steal, kill and destroy. Those are the hallmarks of the devil. He has come to steal your health, to kill you, if you let him, and destroy everything you have. When you get symptoms of illness it is really the devil trying to steal your health. He comes to steal, kill and destroy. He'll take anything he can get his dirty hands on and he couldn't care less what happens to you in the process.

Jesus, on the other hand, has come that you may have life to the full or in abundance. 'Abundance' literally means 'more than enough' - more than enough good health. We can sum up this truth very simply like this:

God good. Devil bad.

Sounds simple doesn't it? But I am always amazed at how many Christians blame God for the bad things that happen in their life. The devil will always try to discredit God in your mind and in your heart. But he is a liar and the father of lies (John 8:44). So let us look at what the Bible says about God being good.

six

God is good!

In the account of creation, in Genesis 1, every day God checked what he had made to make sure it was good. On the final day of creation when he made men and women, he checked to see it was very good. God is concerned that things are good. Goodness is a major priority on God's agenda. God is good.

In Exodus 33:18, Moses says to God, 'Please, show me your glory.'

He was asking to see the mighty glory and presence of the Living God. God's reply is interesting.

He said, 'I will make all my goodness pass before you...' (Exodus 33:19).

The glory of God is his goodness. God is good. In Deuteronomy 28, God lists all the blessings which will come on those people who walk according to his ways. We'll look at those later on.

They are all good. God is good.

David, when writing the psalms, recounted the goodness of God.

'Bless the LORD, O my soul,

And forget not all His benefits:

Who forgives all your iniquities,

Who heals all your diseases,

Who redeems your life from destruction,

Who crowns you with loving kindness and tender mercies,

Who satisfies your mouth with good things,

So that your youth is renewed like the eagle's'

(Psalms 103:2-5).

God heals all your diseases and forgives all your sins. In Exodus God says,

'I am the LORD who heals you.'

(Exodus 15:26).

'But what about Job?' someone says. 'God made him suffer to teach him a lesson didn't he?' If you read the story of Job, you will see that it was Satan who afflicted Job with sickness and brought about the destruction of his family. He was being true to himself - he comes only to steal, kill and destroy (John 10:10). That's what he did to Job.

'Satan went out from the presence of the LORD, and struck Job with painful boils from the sole of his foot to the crown of his head.'

(Job 2:7)

In the closing chapters of that book, it is God who restores Job's health and his possessions. God is good. And Job looks forward to when God's goodness would be revealed in Jesus.

'For I know that my Redeemer lives,
And He shall stand at last on the earth.'

(Job 19:25).

What about Paul's 'thorn in the flesh'? Surely that was an illness sent by God? Again, we need to see what the Bible says. How did Paul describe his thorn in the flesh?

'...a thorn in the flesh was given to me, a messenger of Satan ...' (2 Corinthians 12:7)

We don't know if it was an illness or something else. He doesn't tell us. But we do know that Paul was suffering an attack from Satan and prayed several times for God to remove it, whatever it was. God did say 'my grace is sufficient for you', but God did not put the thorn into Paul's flesh, Satan did. God's advice during the struggle was not to let this attack hold Paul back. By God's grace, Paul would win through and get the victory. Sometimes we have to stand firm through life's battles. When we do, we learn things and grow in spite of the difficulties but God does not send evil on us, the devil does.

God good. Devil bad.

We need to be people who overcome through the power and grace of God. David, meditating on the goodness of God, prophesied,

'Surely goodness and mercy shall follow me all the days of my life;

And I will dwell in the house of the LORD Forever.'

(Psalms 23:6)

My friend, all the scriptures cry out, 'God is good.' Receive that revelation into your spirit. It is the first step to your healing.

seven

Should I expect to be healed?

Yes. And here's why. God decided to enter into a blood covenant with Abraham (Gen 15:17-18).

'On the same day the LORD made a covenant with Abram...'

(Genesis 15:18).

It was a covenant that brought all the blessings outlined in the first half of Deuteronomy 28.

'Blessed shall you be in the city, and blessed shall you be in the country.

Blessed shall be the fruit of your body, the produce of your ground and the increase of your herds, the increase of your cattle and the offspring of your flocks.

Blessed shall be your basket and your kneading bowl.

Blessed shall you be when you come in, and blessed shall you be when you go out.

The Lord will cause your enemies who rise against you to be defeated before your face; they shall come out against you one way and flee before you seven ways.

The Lord will command the blessing on you in your storehouses and in all to which you set your hand, and He will bless you in the land which the Lord your God is giving you.

...And the Lord will grant you plenty of goods, in the fruit of your body, in the increase of your livestock, and in the produce of your ground, in the land of which the Lord swore to your fathers to give you.

The Lord will open to you His good treasure, the heavens, to give the rain to your land in its season, and to bless all the work of your hand.

You shall lend to many nations, but you shall not borrow.

And the Lord will make you the head and not the tail; you shall be above only, and not be beneath...'

(Deuteronomy 28:2-13).

Later on, Jesus came and lived and died to bring you into that same covenant of blessing and peace.

'Christ has redeemed us from the curse of the law, ...that the blessing of Abraham might come upon the Gentiles in Christ Jesus...'

(Galatians 3:13-14).

This covenant of peace is ours if we are in Jesus. The 'Shalom' peace of God carries the meaning of 'nothing broken, nothing missing.' It is our right if we are 'in Christ'.

'Therefore, if anyone is in Christ, he is a new creation; old things have passed away; behold, all things have become new.'

(2 Corinthians 5:17).

Jesus spoke about bringing you into this covenant of blessing at the last supper.

'Then He took the cup, and when He had given thanks He gave it to them, and they all drank from it. And He said to them, 'This is My blood of the new covenant, which is shed for many.''

(Mark 14:23-24)

In the Kingdom of Heaven there can be no sickness and disease. That is why Jesus taught the disciples to pray,

'Your Kingdom come. Your will be done on earth as it is in heaven.'

(Luke 11:2)

Believers are here on the earth primarily to enforce the victory that Jesus has already won for us. It is time to enforce, in your body, the victory that Jesus won for you on the cross.

'He Himself took our infirmities

And bore our sicknesses.'

(Matthew 8:17).

Jesus, on the cross, not only took all the sin of the world upon himself but also all our sickness. He took it into his body so we don't have to accept it in our body. And in reality that is where and when you were healed. The Bible says,

'The punishment that brought us peace was upon him, and by his wounds we are healed.'

(Isaiah 53:5)

That is present tense - we are healed now. Peter goes further.

'...by his wounds you have been healed.'

(1 Peter 2:24)

You were healed when Jesus died on the cross. When you begin to have symptoms of sickness in your body it means Satan is trying to steal the health that Jesus paid for you to have. I don't see myself as being sick. I am healed. Sometimes Satan comes to try and steal my health. I need to rise up as an overcomer and refuse to give Satan any ground in my body.

When Satan attacks, we can find ourselves suddenly in the middle of a storm. The disciples found themselves in the middle of a storm. They were hardened fishermen, used to bad weather. So it must have been a severe storm for them to think they were going to die.

They invited Jesus, who was at peace, sleeping in the boat, to take first place in dealing with the storm. We need to invite Jesus to have first place in our life all the time, so that when the storms of life come they cannot overwhelm us.

If you have never invited Jesus into your life you need to do it now. This is the second step to your healing. Jesus speaks to you now.

'Here I am! I stand at the door and knock. If anyone hears my voice and opens the door, I will come in and eat with him, and he with me.'

(Revelation 3:20).

It is time to welcome Jesus into your life as guest of honour. Find a place where you can be quiet and use the prayer below to invite Jesus into the centre of your life, into your heart, and into any storms that are threatening you at the moment.

Lord Jesus,

Today I want to put my whole life into your hands.

Please forgive me for the past.

For all the bad stuff I have done.

For all the good stuff I didn't do.

I believe you died on the cross for me.

Today I give my life completely to you.

Come into my life today.

I receive you as my Saviour to save me.

I receive you as my Lord to direct me.

I receive you as my Healer to heal me.

Fill me now with your Holy Spirit and teach me from your word.

Thank you Jesus.

I receive you now by faith.

Amen.

eight

Is God a liar?

The next question you need to ask yourself is, 'Do I believe the Bible?' You see we all say 'The truth will set you free.' But the Bible doesn't exactly teach that. I mean the Bible was always true. I had one at home for seventeen years. It was full of truth but it didn't set me free... until I read it and received it. What Jesus actually said was,

'And you shall know the truth, and the truth shall make you free.'

(John 8:32).

We first have to know the truth. Then, as this verse implies, the truth that we know will make us free. I didn't get saved by Jesus until I came to know the truth that he had saved me. I didn't get fully baptised in the Holy Spirit until I came to know the truth about the baptism in the Holy

Spirit. I didn't get anyone healed by God's power until I began to know the truth about healing. Every truth in the Bible will be ineffective until we come to know that truth because it is when we know the truth that the truth sets us free. That is why you must really grasp the truth about healing from God's word, if you want to be healed. The crunch comes, in praying for healing, when we are confronted by God's word. Do we believe it? Many Christians say they believe God's word but they live as though they don't. Yet God's word has power.

'For the word of God is living and powerful, and sharper than any two-edged sword...'

(Hebrews 4:12)

The word of God teaches us that faith is required for healing.

'...the word which they heard did not profit them, not being mixed with faith in those who heard it.'

(Hebrews 4:2)

In almost every incident of healing in the New Testament, we are told that faith was the key issue.

'But Jesus turned around, and when He saw her He said, 'Be of good cheer, daughter; your faith has made you well.' And the woman was made well from that hour.'

(Matthew 9:22)

'Then He touched their eyes, saying, 'According to your faith let it be to you.''

(Matthew 9:29)

'Then Jesus answered and said to her, 'O woman, great is your faith! Let it be to you as you desire.' And her daughter was healed from that very hour.'

(Matthew 15:28).

'When Jesus saw their faith, He said to the paralytic, 'Son, your sins are forgiven you.''

(Mark 2:5)

'And He said to her, 'Daughter, your faith has made you well.''

(Mark 5:34)

'Then Jesus said to him, 'Go your way; your faith has made you well.' And immediately he received his sight ...'

(Mark 10:52)

'Then He said to the woman, 'Your faith has saved you. Go in peace.''

(Luke 7:50)

'But He said to them, 'Where is your faith?' And they were afraid, and marvelled, saying to one another, 'Who can this be? For He commands even the winds and water, and they obey Him!'

(Luke 8:25)

'And He said to her, 'Daughter, be of good cheer; your faith has made you well. Go in peace.'

(Luke 8:48)

'And He said to him, 'Arise, go your way. Your faith has made you well.'

(Luke 17:19)

'Then Jesus said to him, 'Receive your sight; your faith has made you well.'

(Luke 18:42)

Faith is the key that releases healing into your body.

nine

What is faith?

The letter to the Hebrews says,

'Now faith is the substance of things hoped for, the evidence of things not seen.'

(Hebrews 11:1)

Notice that faith is substance. It is the 'stuff' that brings about the miracle. Miracles need some substance. Faith is the substance. It is the currency of the Kingdom of God. Jesus operated his entire ministry on this principle of faith in God's promises. And his faith ministry produced substance that affected the lives of countless millions and still does so today.

'...God anointed Jesus of Nazareth with the Holy Spirit and with power, who went about doing good and healing all who were oppressed by the devil, for God was with Him.' (Acts 10:38).

Clearly faith is the key to healing miracles. So how do we get that miracle-working faith? The answer is that the word of God will give us the faith we need for our healing.

> '...faith comes by hearing, and hearing by the word of God.'

(Romans 10:17)

So the next thing we need to do is settle in our hearts that we will believe what God says about our situation rather than the circumstances. Even when it seems unreasonable to believe God we must settle in our heart to do just that.

> '...let God be true but every man a liar.'

(Romans 3:4)

And we may need to be patient as we wait for faith in God's word to complete its work. We need to add to our faith some patience.

> '...imitate those who through faith and patience inherit the promises.'

(Hebrews 6:12)

We can believe and receive or doubt and go without.

If the word of God says we are healed, we need to align our thinking with God's word not to our problems. And this is where most of us have difficulty.

In our sceptical world where we have been conned and misled many times by advertisers or outright crooks, believing someone's word, when all the circumstances say it cannot be true, can be hard for us. But it is God we are now talking about and he does not lie.

'God is not a man, that He should lie,
Nor a son of man, that He should repent.
Has He said, and will He not do?
Or has He spoken, and will He not make it good?"

(Numbers 23:19).

ten

Our healing begins with our heart.

When we settle in our heart that we will believe God and not the circumstances, that is faith in action. God can easily respond to that sort of faith.

When you begin meditating on the word of God, eventually a seed of truth drops down into your heart. As you allow God's word to grow, you will begin to see yourself differently. You will begin to see that you are healed even though the symptoms may not have changed.

As you begin to think of yourself as healed and believe that to be true - just as God says it is - you will establish that truth in your spirit. Once the truth is established in the spirit, the natural world has to line up with the spirit. Soon healing should appear.

So how can you take authority over your own life and establish the truth about your healing? Jesus used a verse of scripture to establish his own identity with his detractors. It was a verse from Deuteronomy about establishing the truth in a court case. However, Jesus uses it as a biblical principle in all matters of truth.

'by the mouth of two or three witnesses every word may be established.'

(Matthew 18:16)

The devil comes to steal your health. He will often try to put sickness on you and make you own it by the words of your mouth. People talk about 'my asthma', 'my sickness', 'my condition' or whatever. Thus ownership of the sickness is established in the spiritual realm. The devil tells us we are ill by putting symptoms in our body, but he cannot establish that sickness without our assistance. He wants you to say you are ill so he can establish the truth by two witnesses. Most of the time, most of us do just that. We wake up with some symptoms and say 'I think I have the 'flu. I am not well.' We confess with our mouths and believe in our heart and it becomes true. That is how we become a Christian.

'If you confess with your mouth the Lord Jesus and believe in your heart that God has raised Him from the dead, you will be saved.'

(Romans 10:9)

That is how the faith principle basically works.

Confess with your mouth, believe in your heart, and it will come to pass. Jesus said the same about moving mountains.

'For assuredly, I say to you, whoever says to this mountain, 'Be removed and be cast into the sea,' and does not doubt in his heart, but believes that those things he says will be done, he will have whatever he says.'

(Mark 11:23)

'He will have whatever he says,' Jesus said. It is the same principle in action. What comes out of our mouth will affect our health.

'...the tongue of the wise promotes health.'

(Proverbs 12:18)

'Death and life are in the power of the tongue, And those who love it will eat its fruit.'

(Proverbs 18:21).

So how do we apply this principle to sickness? Let me say straight away that it is usually easier to refuse sickness by faith, in the first place, than it is to remove a long-standing sickness. This is because we can only move in proportion to our faith.

'Having then gifts ... let us use them... in proportion to our faith;' (Romans 12:6).

If we have spent a long time believing in our heart and confessing with our mouth that we are sick, we have established faith for sickness. It may require an equal, if not a greater, amount of faith - confessing God's word and believing it in our heart - before we get the breakthrough. Although, under a powerful healing anointing breakthroughs can come very quickly.

eleven

The keys to your healing.

In the Bible, Jesus gives us the keys to the Kingdom. He said that those who believed in him would do the things he had been doing and even greater things. In John's gospel, Jesus gives us the key to seeing miracles in our own life. He was disputing with the Pharisees about his claims to be the Son of God. He said, 'It is also written in your law that the testimony of two men is true.'(John 8:17). I believe Jesus was referring to Deuteronomy 19:15 which is about not condemning an accused murderer to death on the testimony of only one witness.

But here in John's gospel, Jesus teaches that the testimony of two men establishes the truth. I believe this is the key to your healing, your provision and your right to a peaceful life.

In John 10:10 Jesus tells us Satan's plan for your life. He wants to steal, kill and destroy. He wants you in poverty, he wants you sick and he wants you dead. But then Jesus says that He has come that you might have life in abundance.

Every day Satan declares lies about you. Every day God declares blessings on your life. Satan says you are sick and dying. God says you are healed and not in decline. But each of those arguments only has one witness. By themselves neither is valid, nor has any power. They both need a second witness. Now Satan will not change. He hates you. If you love him, he will still hate you. If you hate him, he will hate you. God loves you. He will not change. If you love him he will love you. If you hate him, he will still love you. God and Satan are not going to change.

But you can change and align yourself with God's declaration rather than Satan's. So as you step out of bed in the morning, the evil Satan has planned and the good God has planned are both waiting for a second witness to establish the truth. Satan says, 'It's Monday morning, you hate Mondays. Everything always goes wrong.' If you keep getting out of bed and saying, 'It's Monday morning, I hate Mondays. Everything always goes wrong', you begin to establish the truth by two witnesses.

God, on the other hand, says, 'Goodness and mercy will follow you all the days of your life.' (Psalm 23). If you get out of bed and say, 'Goodness and mercy will follow me all the days of my life,' you begin to establish the truth by two witnesses.

Satan is a liar and the father of lies (John 8:44). He says you are sick. God says of Jesus, 'He took up our infirmities and carried our diseases.' (Matthew 8:17) and 'By his wounds we are healed.' (Isaiah 53:5). Satan says we are sick. God says we are healed. Both wait to be established by a second witness. Do I believe what God says, or what Satan says?

In Romans 3:4, Paul says, 'Let God be true and every man a liar.' Despite the circumstances or symptoms, I choose to believe what God says about me. If God says I am healed, I agree with God even if the circumstances and symptoms contradict God. As I begin to agree with God, I will establish the truth in the spirit. Once something has been established in the spirit, the natural world will begin to line up with it. Your healing should soon manifest itself.

For every situation we face, we need to find God's promise and begin to come into agreement with God. As we do, we will establish God's will in our lives. Never again will we have to pray that stupid prayer 'If it be your will that I am healed....'

The Bible says, 'For all the promises of God in Him are Yes, and in Him Amen, to the glory of God through us.' (2 Corinthians 1:2)

Jesus never said to a sick person, 'Sorry I can't heal you, it's not my Father's will.' God has not only declared that he wants you to be healed, but you were healed when Jesus died on the cross for you. (Matt 8:17, Isa 53.5).

twelve

All things are possible.

Every year, in our ministry, we do something that seems to be the biggest thing we've ever done. But every year God calls us to take a bigger step of faith. We could agree with Satan and say, 'It's impossible.' But we choose to agree with God with whom 'all things are possible.' (Mark 10:27).

As I stood in Nigeria some years ago, preaching to more than seven thousand people, I looked out over the crowd. I began to imagine what would happen if everyone there in that meeting, grasped the full potential of coming into agreement with the word of God and began to refuse to accept the circumstances they were in. What would happen to that nation and to the world if such a number of people reached out and grasped the full potential of 'Christ in you the hope of glory!'? (Col 1:27)

Today, you can rise up and begin coming into agreement with God. You can forbid your lips to speak those negative words, 'I am sick and tired...'

'It makes me sick...' Don't say those things any more. Say, 'By His wounds I am healed.' Say, 'Goodness and mercy will follow me all the days of my life.' Say, 'I can do all things through Christ who strengthens me.' And then watch the miracles happen before your eyes.

thirteen

Child-like faith.

One of the obstacles to receiving a healing is the sheer cynicism and blatant unbelief that pervades so much of British society. And it affects many in the churches too. We need to become like small children again and receive the goodness of God freely.

'Assuredly, I say to you, whoever does not receive the kingdom of God as a little child will by no means enter it.'

(Mark 10:15)

If we don't receive God's word like a little child, we will by no means enter into our healing. The devil is probably already telling you that this book is not true, but you can see that it is firmly based on God's word. Choose to receive it as a small child would.

fourteen

God's Prescription

There is a medicine for your body that can cure every disease and sickness known to man. It has no harmful side effects even when taken in large doses. And when taken daily, as directed, it can prevent sickness and keep you in good health all the time. It is the medicine of God's word.

My [child], give attention to my words;
Incline your ear to my sayings.
Do not let them depart from your eyes;
Keep them in the midst of your heart;
For they are life to those who find them,
And health to all their flesh.'

(Proverbs 4:20-22)

So now meditate on what God says about your health. Put aside what the doctor says and what your body says, for a moment, and let these words of God sink deep into your spirit. Our target is to read God's word slowly, meditating on each phrase. Hear God speaking to you personally in your spirit, through his word.

Healing scripture meditation

Here are some scripture meditations made personal to you with the references of the scriptures on which they are based. Say them out loud and repeat each line several times as you meditate on them

'...only speak a word, and my servant will be healed.'

(Matthew 8:8)

'Bless the LORD, O my soul,

And forget not all His benefits:

Who forgives all my iniquities,

Who heals all my diseases,

Who redeems my life from destruction,

Who crowns me with loving kindness and tender mercies,

Who satisfies my mouth with good things,

So that my youth is renewed like the eagle's.'

(Psalms 103:2-5).

'I am the LORD who heals you.'

(Exodus 15:26).

'by his stripes we are healed.'

(Isaiah 53:5).

'Your healing shall spring forth speedily.'
(Isaiah 58:8).

'For I will restore health to you

And heal you of your wounds,' says the LORD.'
(Jeremiah 30:17).

'When evening had come, they brought to him many ... and with a word he... healed all who were sick.' (Matthew 8:16).

'He Himself took my infirmities

And bore my sicknesses." (Matthew 8:17).

'and they were all healed.' (Acts 5:16).

'by [his] stripes you were healed.' (1 Peter 2:24).

fifteen

Invest in the bank of faith.

Faith needs to become a lifestyle. If you are ever going to move off Mount Average and into the Land of Promise, faith must become a lifestyle. The word of God must be on your lips daily. You know the saying, 'You are what you eat.' There is some truth in that. Sometimes we eat nuts...

What we put into our lives is what we get out. If we keep eating junk food we get a heap of junk for a body. This is true for the body as well as for the spirit. Our spirit affects our body.

'Beloved, I pray that you may prosper in all things and be in health, just as your soul prospers.'

(3 John 1:2)

Your health is affected by how your soul prospers. If you feed your soul with the good stuff your health will improve. The same is true of your body. Food is known to affect our mood and our energy levels. Feed your body with the good stuff and you will affect your health for the better and have more energy.

My wife goes to the gym several mornings a week or swims twenty lengths of the swimming pool before she goes to work. I see people jogging around town dripping in sweat. Some of us can't imagine ourselves ever doing that. For some of us, sudden violent exertion could be dangerous.

James F Fixx, the man who told the world that jogging could stave off heart attacks, died in 1984, of a heart attack, while out jogging.

But there are simple, healthy exercise strategies that we can put in place. Personally, I try to go for a walk for one hour most days, occasionally extending the walk to an hour and a half, about six miles or so. But it means doing things differently and changing what we do.

One definition of insanity is doing the same thing but expecting a different outcome. Many of us have been doing the same things in our eating and drinking habits and in our exercise or lack of it, yet expecting things to change in our health. But that is insane.

There are steps ordinary people like you and me can take to have a healthy spiritual life and a healthy body.

sixteen

The Don Egan Health Plan!

I list here some things that we can all do that will
make a difference to our health. You may not be
able to do all of these every day but you should
attempt to do them all over the period of a week.
Most of them can be done every day if you set your
mind to it.

1. Speak the word of God over your life.

2. Worship.

3. Hear the word.

4. Read the word.

5. Prayer, Exercise and Solitude

6. What are you eating?

1. Speak the word of God over your life.

I strongly recommend you do this every day
if you can. You know, when you are expecting
someone for dinner, you don't wait until they arrive

before you start cooking. You begin preparing well before they arrive because you are expecting them. If you are expecting a healing, you mustn't wait until you are ill to start stirring up your faith. You need to make preparations beforehand, so that when Satan tries to put sickness on you, you are well prepared to overcome his attack by faith in God's word. Then you won't even get sick in the first place.

Faith comes by hearing the word of God (Romans 10:17). We need to speak the word of God out loud with confidence if we are ever going to believe it can affect our life.

'...God... calls those things which be not as though they were.' (Romans 4:17, KJV).

God called Abraham the 'father of many nations' yet he and Sarah were actually childless. But as Abraham accepted his new name and spoke it out, he did become the father of many nations. It wasn't positive thinking, it was confessing things which God had said, but were not, as though they were.

As we confess God's truth over our life we sow a seed in our heart which grows in the spirit, and eventually produces a harvest of health and healing. Stop listening to what your body says, or what your fears say, and start listening to what God says about you. Use this exercise to develop your faith and to help you see that you were healed when Jesus died on the cross 2000 years ago. You are now enforcing the victory that Jesus has already won for you in your body.

Here is a confession for you to use every day. You can use other scriptures as you study the word and speak them over yourself to bless you. Speak it out loud, confidently asserting that what God has said about you is what is really true. Remember that we may be calling those things that are not as though they were (Rom 4:17).

Daily Faith Confession

Father, I thank you that I am your child and that you brought me into your kingdom through the Blood Covenant of Jesus.

Through his cross you redeemed me that the blessing of Abraham might come upon me. (Galatians 3:14)

I receive the gift of the Holy Spirit.

As I speak your word I will be healed. (Matthew 8:8)

I bless you Lord and remember all your benefits:

you forgive all my iniquities,

you heal all my diseases,

you redeem my life from destruction,

you crown me with loving kindness and tender mercies,

you satisfy my mouth with good things,

so that my youth is renewed like the eagle's.

Yes, my youth is renewed like the eagle's. (Psalms 103:2-5).

You are the Lord who heals me. (Exodus 15:26)

By your wounds I am healed. (Isaiah 53:5)

My healing shall spring forth quickly. (Isaiah 58:8)

You will restore health to me and heal me of my wounds. (Jeremiah 30:17).

Your will is to heal all who are sick. (Matthew 8:16)

You yourself took my infirmities and bore my sicknesses so I don't have to. (Matthew 8:17)

Thank you Lord that I am not the sick trying to get well, but the healed, from whom Satan is trying to steal health.

I refuse you, Satan, you have no authority in my life.

I belong to Jesus.

Jesus, the Anointed One, and his anointing live in me.

I receive my healing now by faith in every part of my body, mind and spirit.

Thank you Father. I am healed in Jesus' name. Amen.

2. Worship.

I don't know what stirs your spirit into worship. Be it an old hymn or the latest song from Hill-songs Australia, put a CD in the machine, at home or in the car and worship God loudly. Singing out praises to God fervently does release something good in the spirit. It sweeps away the negativity and the pity parties we often attend for ourselves. Whatever our problem is, we need to praise God with our body, mind and spirit. He is bigger than all our problems put together. As we praise God with all our heart, we begin to shift the focus of our attention from the problem to the solution. David did the same thing as a young boy. He moved the focus from the intimidating Goliath to the Living God, who is far bigger.

3. Hear the word.

Listen to some good preaching. Get a CD or a download of some good faith-filled preaching. Take some notes. Many people belittle preaching as boring and indeed, some of it is. But faith comes by hearing the word of God and if we can hear the passion of a faith-filled preacher, it can stir our spirits up to faith. One church told a visiting preacher they liked ten-minute sermons. They told him so many times before he preached he gave them three ten minute sermons all in one go! Don't leave preaching for Sunday only. Preaching of the word is healing to our bodies.

'My son, give attention to my words;

Incline your ear to my sayings.

Do not let them depart from your eyes;

Keep them in the midst of your heart;

For they are life to those who find them,

And health to all their flesh.'

(Proverbs 4:20-22).

I could just say, 'read your Bible', but many of us are not very excited by that. We need a preacher to teach us about God's word and stir us up to faith.

4. Read the word.

Read some teaching on faith. You may not be a great reader but you can read a chapter of a good teaching book every day or so. If you don't know of any, may I suggest my some of my other books available from www.rsvptrust.co.uk or Amazon for a quick faith lift.

5. Prayer, Exercise and Solitude

- One hour prayer walk.

I prayer walk for an hour, several times a week. I walk about four or five miles in a circular route from home. This is good for me for several reasons. It is good exercise which promotes good health. At first, it seemed like a marathon but now it seems very short. It creates a space for solitude and reflection. I know I can pray and, whatever the distractions, I can't give up and forget it because I still have to walk home! I always spend an hour in prayer on an hour-long prayer walk - it can't fail. It also creates space and solitude.

6. What are you eating?

I am no nutritionist but it is common knowledge that what we eat affects our mood and our energy levels. Recently, by changing what I eat very slightly, I have been able to have a steady flow of energy all day, instead of the boom and bust energy rollercoaster, with its accompanying weariness, that I used to have through eating too much sugar.

Some foods have cancer preventing properties. Some have cancer inducing properties. Isn't it worth finding out what natural things will promote healing and health to our bodies? We don't have to be slimming to put some thought into our diet. Nor does it need to be boring.

A book I have found very helpful is *'The Food Doctor - Healing foods for Mind and Body'* by Vicki Edgson and Ian Marber (Published by Collins & Brown ISBN 1-85585-682-4) and I recommend it to you.

sixteen

Relationships can help...

In addition to these things we need to develop healthy relationships. These, too, will help our health.

Friendship.

Be with others. Friendships can be healing. Join a sports club together. Go surfing. Go ten pin bowling. Do something you've never done. Be imaginative. Live a little!

'And the LORD God said, 'It is not good that man should be alone; I will make him a helper comparable to him.'

(Genesis 2:18)

I love solitude and space but it is not good for us to be alone too much. We need a close friend. It should be a relationship where we give as well as receive. Some people are lonely because they suck everyone dry by making them listen to all their problems. Healthy relationships are always two-way, where both people give and receive.

If you are married you need to invest in the relationship with your spouse. Usually, when I do an extended walk for a couple of hours, my wife Hazel comes with me. Now our children are older that is getting easier to arrange. We've begun a second courtship over recent years, doing new things together, just the two of us. It's been wonderful.

'...rejoice with the wife of your youth.' (Proverbs 5:18).

If you're single you can still develop a close friendship where you can feel safe sharing in a personal way.

Soul Friends.

'As iron sharpens iron,
So a man sharpens the countenance of his friend.'

(Proverbs 27:17)

It's good for a man to have a man to share hopes and dreams with, and a woman another woman. I have several friends, mainly people in ministry, who bless me by 'sharpening my countenance'. We certainly don't agree on everything but that is how 'iron sharpens iron.' Soul friends can be two people playing sport, sharing a hobby or interest where the relationship is mutually beneficial.

It is the reason pubs are so popular - because men find an undemanding yet challenging relationship with other men very helpful.

All these things, integrated into your daily life, will begin to affect your health and healing for the better. Spirituality does require discipline.

Disciple and discipline come from the same root word.

seventeen

Moving mountains.

'For assuredly, I say to you, whoever says to this mountain, 'Be removed and be cast into the sea,' and does not doubt in his heart, but believes that those things he says will be done, he will have whatever he says.'

(Mark 11:23)

Jesus says that if we have faith the size of a mustard seed, we will be able to move mountains (Matthew 17:20). Sometimes a sickness seems like a mountain. It seems immovable and a lot bigger than we are. But Jesus says we can move such things and make them disappear if we apply the faith principle of speaking and believing God's word.

We have power to command things to happen if we have been born again into the Kingdom of

God. Jesus says that if we say to the problem 'Be removed' and believe in our heart that those things we say will be done, we will have whatever we say. And if we base our commands on God's word we know God will perform such things.

'Then the LORD said '...I am ready to perform My word.'' (Jeremiah 1:12).

That is why we should speak out the daily confession and expect all sickness to be removed.

'This is the confidence we have in approaching God: that if we ask anything according to his will, he hears us. And if we know that he hears us - whatever we ask - we know that we have what we asked of him.'

(1 John 5:14-15)

Most of us want to talk to God *about* the mountain. But Jesus didn't say that. He said speak *to* the mountain and tell it to be removed. Unless we begin to line our faith up with the word of God, we will be frustrated in the area of healing. We will be shooting in the dark, developing our own little theology of healing - win some, lose some. That is not what the word says.

'For all the promises of God in Him are Yes, and in Him Amen, to the glory of God through us.'

(2 Corinthians 1:20)

Romans 3:4 says, '...let God be true but every man a liar...'

We need to be careful what we say. We need to speak the word and speak faith over our bodies. Even when I am well, I recite healing scriptures to my body. I do this to store up faith for the day when attacks on my health may come. If I have been sowing the seed of the word, which produces faith, my harvest of healing will come much quicker. It will also be much more difficult for Satan to put sickness in my body in the first place.

When Jesus healed the sick he didn't 'pray for them'. Instead, he spoke to sick bodies and commanded them to be healed, or declared that they were healed. He told the man who could not stand up, to stand up and walk home. He took authority over the man's body when he saw the faith of the four men who brought him. He said to the waves and the storm on the lake 'Peace, be still!' (Mark 4:39). And it was still. In Mark 5:41 he spoke to a dead girl and told her to get up. And she did. In Mark 9:25 he told a deaf and mute spirit to come out of a boy ... and it did. He taught the disciples to do the same - to speak to sick bodies and command them to be healed, and expect them to be healed.

eighteen

Claim your healing

You see, when God created the world, he used his word. In Genesis 1, he spoke to the darkness and said, 'Let there be light.' And there was light. He made us in his image and gave us dominion over the earth. Restored believers have the power and authority to speak to the natural world in accordance with God's word, and expect it to obey them.

In all of our ministry to the sick, this is the method I use, because this is the method Jesus and the disciples used. I believe that God has already healed people by the blood of Jesus Christ. Their healing is a foregone conclusion. I speak healing scriptures to those gathered. I speak to their bodies and command them to be healed. Hundreds have testified to healing miracles. I have lost count of the number of blind people who have received back their sight as a result of believing Jesus and his word. I have seen lame men leaping and dancing and praising God. I have seen the deaf and mute begin to speak, people with agonising pain become completely pain free. Jesus has paid for their healing with his own blood. All we need to do is come and claim that healing with faith and confidence.

When we claim an inheritance, someone has to die for us to receive it. Some people think we have to wait until we die before we claim our inheritance from God. But Jesus has already died! It is because of his death, not ours, that we come into our inheritance, which includes the healing of our bodies.

God said to Paul that he was sent 'to open their eyes, in order to turn them from darkness to light, and from the power of Satan to God, that they may receive forgiveness of sins and an inheritance among those who are sanctified by faith in me.' (Acts 26:18).

nineteen

A few questions...

Is it a lack of faith if I go to the doctor?

No. We can still believe God for a miracle while getting some relief through medicine. The doctor has the same aim - to heal you. But as you get the victory in your health you will probably visit the doctor less and less, simply because you are well. We are creatures made up of body, mind and spirit. We need to advance the war on sickness on all those fronts.

Should I stop taking my medication - is that faith in action?

If you are on medication from a doctor, I would not recommend that you suddenly stop taking it. If you believe your healing has happened then go to the doctor and let him or her check you over. If your medication can be reduced or stopped altogether your doctor can advise you properly.

Shouldn't I just accept some illness as the onset of old age?

No. Old age is not synonymous with declining health.

'Moses was one hundred and twenty years old when he died. His eyes were not dim nor his natural vigour diminished.'

(Deuteronomy 34:7).

The devil would like you to believe that you will decline rapidly as you get older because he has come to steal kill and destroy. He loves it when you say, 'I think old age is creeping on' when you forget something, so he can establish your decline by the words of your own mouth.

I am believing for the health of Moses right into old age - no dimming of eye sight, no reduction in my 'natural vigour'.

twenty

Jesus lives in you

St Paul wrote, '...God willed to make known what are the riches of the glory of this mystery among the Gentiles: which is Christ in you, the hope of glory." (Colossians 1:27).

If you have invited Jesus to come into your life, then Christ - the Anointed One and his anointing - is in you. That same Jesus who made the blind see and the lame walk, the deaf to hear and the mute to speak, is in you. The same Jesus who walked on water, controlled the weather and raised the dead, lives in the believer. He is nearer to you than your own hands and feet, closer to you than your own breath. It's worth meditating on that for a while.

Inviting Jesus into your heart will affect your whole life. The more you meditate on it and think about 'Christ in you', the more his healing power will flow in your body. The Holy Spirit lives in the body of the believer. The very life source of

Jesus lives in you and releases the benefits of the Kingdom of God as you exercise your faith in Jesus.

'But if the Spirit of Him who raised Jesus from the dead dwells in you, He ...will also give life to your mortal bodies through His Spirit who dwells in you.'

(Romans 8:11)

Many of us wish we could have met Jesus when he was in the flesh. We think a relationship with him through the Holy Spirit is second rate, compared to meeting him in a body face to face. But that is not true. Jesus was with the disciples but he is lives in you.

'But because I have said these things to you, sorrow has filled your heart. Nevertheless, I tell you the truth. It is to your advantage that I go away; for if I do not go away, the Helper will not come to you; but if I depart, I will send Him to you.'

(John 16:6-7)

On the day of Pentecost, that presence and power of God that was in Jesus, came to live in the believers. Before this, he had been with them. Now, he was in them. The very power that Jesus used to make the blind to see, the deaf to hear and the lame to walk, lives in the believer.

'But to you who fear My name
The Sun of Righteousness shall arise
With healing in His wings.'

(Malachi 4:2)

We can hinder the work of the Holy Spirit by opening the door to evil in our lives. The doors to evil are many. Broad is the road that leads to destruction. Stealing, adultery, seances, freemasonry, spiritualism, witchcraft, pornography, hatred, bitterness and unforgiveness are all doors which allow evil to enter our life and inhibit the Holy Spirit. You need to be on first name terms with the Holy Spirit. He is holy.

'Beloved, do not believe every spirit, but test the spirits, whether they are of God; because many false prophets have gone out into the world.'

(1 John 4:1)

If you have been involved in anything which has opened the door to evil you can repent of it and renounce your involvement with it, burn any equipment related to it and God will forgive us and free us up to receive more from him.

'And many who had believed came confessing and telling their deeds.
Also, many of those who had practiced magic brought their books together and burned them in the sight of all. And they counted up the value of

them, and it totalled fifty thousand pieces of silver.
So the word of the Lord grew mightily and
prevailed.'

(Acts 19:18-20)

'If we confess our sins, He is faithful and just
to forgive us our sins and to cleanse us from all
unrighteousness.'

(1 John 1:9)

The more you walk with God in the Spirit, the
more his Kingdom can touch your life and your
body. It comes back to our spiritual diet. What we
put in is what we get out. Jesus put this in a very
radical way.

'I am the living bread which came down from
heaven. If anyone eats of this bread, he will live
forever; and the bread that I shall give is my flesh,
which I shall give for the life of the world.'

(John 6:51)

twenty one

How to pray for healing

Here is a prayer for healing. Use it every day
until your healing manifests itself. Look for other
healing scriptures and memorise them and speak
them over your body even when you are well. Faith
comes by hearing.

*'Is anyone among you sick? Let him call for the
elders of the church, and let them pray over him,
anointing him with oil in the name of the Lord. And
the prayer of faith will save the sick, and the Lord
will raise him up. And if he has committed sins, he
will be forgiven. Confess your trespasses to one
another, and pray for one another, that you may be
healed. The effective, fervent prayer of a righteous
man avails much.'*

(James 5:14-16)

Prayer For Healing

Say this prayer out loud, confidently asserting your position in God's kingdom through the finished work of Jesus.

Father, I thank you that you love me and care for me.

I thank you for sending Jesus.

Jesus, I thank you that you took my infirmities and bore my sicknesses so I don't have to.

You are the Lord who heals me.

And I declare your word over my body now, that by your stripes I am healed.

I declare that Satan is a liar.

That I am not the sick trying to get well, but I am the healed, from whom Satan is trying to steal health.

I refuse you, Satan. I refuse you, sickness.

I will not have you in my body.

I submit myself to God and I resist you devil.

You have to flee from me according to God's word.

It is written, 'Resist the devil and he will flee from you.'

I resist you now in the name of Jesus.

I speak to this mountain of sickness and I command you to leave my body in the name of Jesus.

I take authority over this body in the name of Jesus.

I break every power of sickness affecting this body now.

I receive afresh the blood of Jesus on my life.

I declare that this body belongs to Jesus.

The Anointed One and his anointing live in me.

I break your power, sickness, in the name of Jesus.

Body, I take authority over you in the name of Jesus,

I command you to be healed now, in Jesus' name.

Thank you, Jesus, that you have already paid for this healing on the cross.

I receive my healing now, by faith, in Jesus' name.

I am healed by your stripes. Thank you, Father.

Amen.

Sometimes I use a shorter prayer of faith that would go something like this.

'By his stripes I am healed. He has borne my sicknesses. Sickness, I command you in the name of Jesus to go from my body. I break your power, Satan. You have no right to touch my body with sickness. I am covered by the blood of Jesus. Body, I command you to be healed in the name of Jesus.'

twenty two

Keeping your Healing

In John 10:10 Jesus tells us that Satan is a thief who comes to steal, kill and destroy. Many people have prayed the prayers in this book and have received immediate relief from pain and sickness. Amazingly, a few days later, they find themselves back to square one and say, 'Oh, it didn't really work.'

Actually, it did really work but the thief came to steal their health again and they didn't stand against him in faith. This issue of healing is spiritual warfare - we cannot be half-hearted and expect Satan to run away.

'Resist the devil and he will flee from you.'

(James 4:7)

'Resist him, steadfast in the faith.'

(1 Peter 5:9)

As in normal warfare, a constant bombardment is hard to resist and can make us crumble. That is why we need to constantly bombard Satan with the word of God and our faith in it.

As we resist him in this way, he will crumble. If we don't resist him, we will crumble and give in to sickness.

When I began to get some revelation of healing, Satan attacked my wife with sickness. It was a skin irritation that went on for nearly a year. The doctor was at a loss to explain it. I wondered if I had brought back some strange disease from Africa. We had to keep coming against that illness in faith. The temptation to give up was immense. But it just was not acceptable to resign ourselves to the idea that Hazel would suffer for the rest of her life. We fought on in prayer. Eventually, we discovered it was a rare infection and I am glad to say that Hazel has been well for several years now.

When we receive Jesus as our Lord and Saviour, we trust him in our heart and confess that faith with our mouth. It is a foregone conclusion that we will get to heaven because of receiving what Jesus did for us on the cross. That is our confident expectation.

We must adopt this attitude in the area of healing as well. And when we receive a healing through believing and speaking God's word, we must keep that healing the same way.

'As you have therefore received Christ Jesus the Lord, so walk in Him.'

(Colossians 2:6)

If the symptoms come back, have some warfare with Satan through God's word in your mouth. Notice that in the temptation of Jesus, he overcame Satan with the word of God. Every time he replied to the devil's attacks he said, 'It is written...' and then quoted from the Bible. (Matthew 4). If Jesus needed to speak the word of God to get the victory, how much more do we.

I strongly suggest you re-read this book over and over until that faith in God's word drops into your heart. God bless you as you believe God for your complete healing in body, mind and spirit.

twenty three

Write to me

I would love to hear from you if you have a testimony of a healing breakthrough where this little book has been of help or you have received personal ministry in one of our services. As we share our testimony, it releases more power for us to overcome the enemy.

'And they overcame him by the blood of the Lamb and by the word of their testimony.'

(Revelation 12:11)

Please drop me a line today through the post or by email if you have that. The details are below. It would be a great encouragement to hear from you today.

Also if you would like to receive our RSVP Newsletter by email you can sign up on our website www.rsvptrust.co.uk

'The LORD bless you and keep you;
The LORD make His face shine upon you,
And be gracious to you;
The LORD lift up His countenance upon you,
And give you peace.'

(Numbers 6:24-26)

Contact me at:

Don Egan

P O Box 55

STOWMARKET

Suffolk

IP14 1UG

or contact us through our website:

www.rsvptrust.co.uk

Please also rate this book on Amazon as that really helps me get the message out.

Other books by Don Egan

Healing is coming!

The sequel to *A word about your healing* is out now! A completely new book on healing through Christ. Answering many frequently asked questions and with prayers for healing and simple guide to being healed and praying for others.

With chapters on the roots of sickness, the source of healing, healing of the body, healing of the heart and healing of the soul, this new book explores the subject of Christian healing in detail - all in Don's down to earth style.

Available now from RSVP Trust, P O Box 55, Stowmarket, Suffolk, IP14 1UG.

Or online at:

www.rsvptrust.co.uk

Printed in Great Britain
by Amazon